Come Into The Garden Maud

A Light Comedy

Noël Coward

A SAMUEL FRENCH ACTING EDITION

SAMUEL FRENCH

FOUNDED 1830

SAMUELFRENCH-LONDON.CO.UK
SAMUELFRENCH.COM

FOR AMATEUR PRODUCTION ENQUIRIES

UNITED KINGDOM AND WORLD EXCLUDING NORTH AMERICA

plays@SamuelFrench-London.co.uk

020 7255 4302/01

Each title is subject to availability from Samuel French,

depending upon country of performance.

COME INTO THE GARDEN MAUD

Produced by H. M. Tennent Ltd, at the Queen's Theatre, London, on the 25th April 1966, with the following cast of characters:

(in order of their appearance)

ANNA-MARY CONKLIN	*Irene Worth*
FELIX, a waiter	*Seán Barrett*
VERNER CONKLIN	*Noël Coward*
MAUD CARAGNANI	*Lilli Palmer*

The play directed by VIVIAN MATALON
Setting by BRIAN CURRAH

SCENE

*The action of the play passes in a
private suite in the Hotel Beau Rivage, Lausanne-Ouchy,
in Switzerland*

Time—the present. An evening in summer

COME INTO THE GARDEN MAUD

Scene 1

Scene—*The sitting-room of a private suite of a luxurious hotel in Switzer-land. Seven o'clock on an evening in early summer.*

Down L *is a door opening into the bedroom. There are double doors up slightly* L *of* C *which open into a small lobby, from which open other rooms and the corridor. The windows leading on to a balcony* R *are open, dis-closing a view of the lake of Geneva with the mountains of France on the opposite shore.*

When the CURTAIN *rises,* ANNA-MARY CONKLIN *is sitting* L *on the sofa, her feet up, polishing her nails. Standing* C *between the sofa and the arm-chair is* FELIX, *a handsome floor waiter.* ANNA-MARY CONKLIN *is an exceedingly wealthy American matron in her late forties or early fifties. At the moment she is wearing an elaborate blue peignoir, blue ostrich-feather "mules" and a hair-net through which can be discerned blue hair tortured in the grip of a number of metal curlers. Her expression is disagreeable because she happens to be talking to a member of the lower classes.*

ANNA-MARY. And another thing young man. When I ask for a bottle of Evian water *bien* glacée to be put by my bed every night, I *mean* a bottle of Evian water *bien* glacée and not a bottle of Perrier water which is not glacée at all, and *gazouze* into the bargain.

FELIX. I am most sorry, Madame. It shall not occur again.

ANNA-MARY. And you might also explain to that chambermaid, Caterina or whatever her damn name is, that for my breakfast I take prune juice, not orange juice, toast Melba and not rolls, and good American coffee served with cream, not that thick black French stuff served with lukewarm milk.

FELIX. Very well, Madame.

ANNA-MARY. And you can tell her as well that I don't like being nattered at the first thing in the morning in a language that I can't understand. Neither Mr Conklin nor I speak a word of Italian and the sooner the staff of this hotel realizes it, the better it will be for everybody concerned.

FELIX (*blandly*) Va bene, Signora.

ANNA-MARY. Are you being impertinent?

FELIX. Oh no, Madame. I most humbly beg your pardon. It's just a question of habitude.

ANNA-MARY. It may interest you to know that Mr Conklin and I have stayed in most of the finest hotels in Europe, and when we pay the amount we do pay for the best service, we expect to get it.

FELIX. Very good, Madame.
ANNA-MARY. That will be all for the moment.

(FELIX *moves towards the doors*)

You'd better bring some ice later. Mr Conklin takes his Scotch with lots of ice and plain water.
FELIX. Madame.
ANNA-MARY. Is the water here all right?
FELIX (*puzzled*) I fear I do not quite understand, Madame.
ANNA-MARY. The drinking water? I mean it isn't just pumped up out of that lake without being properly filtered?
FELIX. There have been no complaints as far as I know, Madame.
ANNA-MARY. All right—you can go now.
FELIX (*bowing*) A votre service, Madame.

(FELIX *exits up* C. ANNA-MARY *rises and goes to the telephone on the table above the sofa*)

ANNA-MARY (*into the receiver*) Hallo . . . Operator . . . Ici Mrs Conklin . . . Oui, Mrs Verner Conklin, suite three-five-four. Voulez-vous me donner le numero de André's, le coiffeur? . . . No, I don't know the number; that's why I'm asking you for it—the place is way up in the town somewhere not far from that big bridge. I was there this afternoon . . . All right, I'll hold on. (*There is a pause while she examines her nails with distaste. Then she continues in her execrable French accent*) 'Allo—Je voudrai parler avec Monsieur André lui-meme . . . Oui, de la part de Mrs Conklin . . . Pardon—il est parti? (*She sits* R *on the sofa with her feet up*) Vous parlez Anglais? . . . Oh, bon. Well, I'd like you to tell Monsieur André from me that the girl he gave me this afternoon has absolutely ruined my nails. I asked for Carmine foncée and what I got is tangerine foncée and they look terrible. I never noticed until I got out into the daylight. I had to take the stuff all off—and what is more she cut my cuticles, and if there's one thing I can't stand it is to have my cuticles cut; I like them pushed back gently with an orange stick—and you can also explain to him that when I say I want a blue rinse I *mean* a blue rinse and not a purple dye. I've been under the shower for forty minutes trying to tone it down and . . . What? . . . Well, I can't help who you are— (*Rising to the table, and putting the telephone down*) — you just give him those messages from Mrs Conklin . . . Yes Conklin —C o n k l i n. Thank you. (*She replaces the receiver, takes a cigarette from a box on the table, lights it, then picks up the receiver again*) 'Allo, 'allo—Operator—donnez moi vingt trois—trent six—vingt deux . . . Merci. . . . 'Allo—'Allo—Ici Mrs Conklin—je veux parler avec la comtesse s'il vous plait . . . Oui—Conklin . . . 'Allo—Mariette? . . . Yes, it's me—Anna-Mary! . . . Why, it's just wonderful to hear your voice. I can't believe we're actually here at last; I just keep pinching myself. I tried to call you this morning but your number was busy. First of all I want to thank you for those gorgeous flowers, it was just darling of you to send us such a lovely welcome—my dear, they light up the whole room, they literally do—I'm looking at them this very minute. . . . Oh, Verner? He's all right; he's out playing golf somewhere, as usual. (*She sits on the* L *arm of the sofa*) Now listen, honey, about tonight—you know about the etiquette of these sort of things much better than I do—ought I to go outside and *wait* for the Prince or will it be all right to have him sent to the bar where we're having cocktails? . . . Oh—he likes things to be informal? Well, all I can say is thank God for that, because I simply wouldn't know how to be anything else—I don't have to curtsy to her, too, do I? . . . I do? Whatever for? I mean she was only a commoner after all before he married her . . . Oh, I see. Very well, I'll do what you say, but for heaven's sakes get here early to give me moral support . . . You're an angel! How's dear Henri? . . . Out playing golf, too! Well, I suppose it gives them something to do. Au revoir, darling—a ce soir.

(ANNA-MARY *replaces the receiver, picks up her sponge-bag from the sofa and exits down* L. *As soon as she has gone* VERNER CONKLIN *enters up* C. *He is a tall, pleasant-looking man in his late fifties. There is little remarkable about him beyond the fact that he has spent the major portion of his life making a great deal of money. He is carrying a bag of golf-clubs which he flings down on the sofa. He turns* C.
ANNA-MARY *enters* L)

(*Ominously*) So you're back, are you?
VERNER. Yeah, sweetheart.
ANNA-MARY. You know, Verner, try as I may I just *do not* understand you.
VERNER (*taking a cigarette from the box on the table* C *and lighting it*) What's wrong?
ANNA-MARY. Well, to start with it's past six o'clock **and** we've got to be down in the bar and dressed by eight.
VERNER. What for? You said nobody was coming before eight-thirty.
ANNA-MARY. Did you remember about the cigars?
VERNER. Yes, I remembered about them.
ANNA-MARY. Well, thank heaven for small mercies.
VERNER. But the store was shut.
ANNA-MARY (*exasperated*) Verner!
VERNER. Sorry, sweetheart.
ANNA-MARY. Why didn't you call in on the way *out* to the golf-course?
VERNER. I did. That was when the store was shut.
ANNA-MARY (*turning away*) I only have to ask you to do the smallest thing . . .

VERNER. All the stores shut in this lousy town from twelve until three.

ANNA-MARY. Clare Pethrington told me that the Prince likes a special sort of cigar which can only be got at one particular place here, and I, thinking it would be a nice gesture to have them served to him after dinner, am fool enough to ask you to take care of it for me—and what happens?

VERNER. Nothing happens. He does without 'em.

ANNA-MARY. Now look here, Verner . . .

VERNER. There's no sense in working yourself up into a snip. I guess the cigars you get in this hotel are liable to be good enough for anybody, and if His Royal Highness doesn't fancy 'em he can smoke his own, can't he? (*He sits on the* L *arm of the sofa*)

ANNA-MARY (*moving to* L *of the sofa, bitterly*) You wouldn't care if the first dinner-party we gave in this "lousy town" as you call it, were a dead failure, would you?

VERNER. Calm down, sweetheart—it won't be. Our parties ain't ever failures; they cost too damn much.

ANNA-MARY. You know, Verner, that's one of the *silliest* things I've ever heard you say. The sort of people we're entertaining to-night are interested in other things besides money.

VERNER. Like hell they are!

ANNA-MARY (*moving down* L) I can't think what you came on this trip for. (*She sits down* L *and puts out her cigarette*) You can play golf in Minneapolis.

VERNER. And on a damn sight better course, too.

ANNA-MARY. You just about sicken me, Verner, you really do. Don't you get any kick at all out of travelling to new places and meeting distinguished people?

VERNER. What's so distinguished about 'em?

ANNA-MARY. Wouldn't you consider a royal Prince distinguished?

VERNER. How do I know? I haven't met him yet.

ANNA-MARY. He just happens to be one of the most fascinating men in Europe, and one of the most sought after.

VERNER. Except in his own country, which he got thrown out of.

ANNA-MARY. You make me ashamed, saying things like that.

VERNER. Listen, sweetheart. Hows about you just stopping balling me out and ringing for some ice? I want a drink.

ANNA-MARY. Ring for it yourself.

VERNER (*equably, rising*) Okay—okay. (*He rings the bell up* LC)

(*The telephone rings.* ANNA-MARY *rises to answer it*)

ANNA-MARY. Hallo? . . . What? Who? . . . She's on her way up? Thank you. (*She hangs up*) Oh my God!

VERNER. What's wrong?

Anna-Mary. It's Maud—Maud Caragnani. I invited her to come and have a drink, and it went completely out of my head.

Verner (*sitting* c) Well, we'll give her a drink. We can afford it.

Anna-Mary. Here am I with so much on my mind that I'm going crazy, and all you can do is try to be funny.

Verner. Sorry, sweetheart.

Anna-Mary. And take those dirty old golf-clubs off the couch. This is a private sitting-room, not the hotel lobby.

Verner. I'll take 'em away when I've had my drink. She's the one we had dinner with that night in Rome, isn't she?

Anna-Mary (*moving down* l *and sitting*) She certainly is, in that stuffy little apartment that smelled of fish. (*She polishes her nails*) I thought I'd die. No air-conditioning and all those ghastly stairs.

Verner. I thought it was quite a cute little place, kinda picturesque. I liked her, too. As a matter of fact, she was the only one we met in Rome that I did like.

Anna-Mary (*with an unpleasant little laugh*) Only because she made a play for you. Why, she practically threw herself at your head; it would have been embarrassing if it hadn't been so funny. I remember catching Lulu Canfield's eye across the table and it was as much as we could do not to burst out laughing.

Verner. Well, it made a change, anyway. Most of the characters we seem to pick up along the line don't even trouble to speak to me.

Anna-Mary. You've only got yourself to blame for that, Verner. It's just that you happen to be a "taker" and not a "giver". You won't make an *effort* with people. You just sit there looking grouchy and don't say a word.

Verner. Maybe. But I do say the five most important words of the evening. "Garcon—bring me the cheque!"

Anna-Mary. You know something, Verner? It's just that very attitude of mind that makes Europeans despise us Americans. Can't you think of anything but dollars and cents?

Verner (*mildly*) They're my dollars and cents, sweetheart, and I've spent the best part of my life pilin' 'em up, and if there didn't happen to be a hell of a lot of 'em you can bet your sweet ass we shouldn't be sitting here worrying about special cigars for Royal Princes and giving dinner-parties to people who despise us.

Anna-Mary. I wish you wouldn't use vulgar expressions like that.

Verner. And I'll tell you something else. This dame who's on her way up, the one that handed you and Lulu Canfield such a good laugh by "throwing herself at my head", she at least took the trouble to give *us* dinner.

Anna-Mary (*rising and crossing* r *to put her cotton wool in the waste-paper-basket*) Of course she did. It was a sprat to catch a whale. Even I could see that. She hasn't got a cent to her name. She's one of those social parasites who go about living off rich people.

VERNER. Well, at least she can't be lonely. The woods are full of 'em. Anyway, if you think so badly of her, why the hell did you ask her round for a drink?

ANNA-MARY (*moving to* C) After all, she knows everybody, and she goes everywhere. She phoned me this morning, and I had to think of something.

VERNER. She happens to be a Princess, too, doesn't she? That's always a help.

ANNA-MARY. Only a Sicilian one. Princes in Sicily are a dime a dozen. My God, I can't receive her looking like this! (*Moving* L) I must put something in my hair.

VERNER. Try a crash-helmet, sweetheart. You're sure in a fighting mood.

(ANNA-MARY *shoots him a withering glance and exits hurriedly into the bedroom* L. VERNER *rises and puts the golf-bag behind the* L *end of the sofa. There is a knock at the door.* VERNER *goes and opens it, standing* R *of it.* MAUD CARAGNANI *enters. She is an attractive-looking woman of about forty-seven or eight. Her appearance is a trifle baroque. She has style, but it is a style that is entirely her own. She wears no hat, and a number of heavy gold bracelets. She is English born and bred, and has acquired much of the jargon of what is known as "The International Set." Beneath this, however, she is a woman of considerable intelligence. She puts her bag on the desk up* RC *and greets Verner by taking both his hands in hers*)

MAUD. It's lovely to see you again, Verner. I hoped you'd be here, but I wasn't sure. Anna-Mary sounded a bit "affolée" on the telephone this morning. I gather she's giving a dinner-party this evening for our portly Prince.

VERNER. Do you know the guy?

MAUD. Oh yes, he's a horror. (*She sits on the* L *arm of the sofa*)

(VERNER *closes the door, then comes to above the* C *chair*)

A great one for lavatory jokes and a bit of bottom-pinching on the side. The new wife's quite sweet and lovely to look at; she used to be a model, I believe. He insists on everyone bobbing to her and when they do she's liable to giggle. You'll like her.

VERNER. Did Anna-Mary ask you tonight?

MAUD. Yes, a little half-heartedly, I thought. (*She laughs*) Not that I blame her; she's probably got all the "placements" set. In any case, I couldn't possibly have come even if I had wanted to. I'm driving back to Rome.

VERNER. It's a hell of a long trip. Are you driving yourself?

MAUD. Oh yes. I love driving alone, particularly at night. I shall see the dawn come up over the Simplon pass and probably get as far as Como for breakfast.

Verner. What kind of a car?

Maud. Rather a common little Volkswagen, you know, the type that looks as if it were sticking its tongue out, but it goes like a bird.

Verner (*admiringly*) You certainly are quite a gal!

(Felix *enters up* c *with an ice-bucket on a tray*)

Felix. Buona sera, Principesa.

Maud. Buona sera, Felix. Come sta?

Felix. Molto bene, grazie, e lie?

Maud. Bene come sempre. Partiro stanotte a Roma.

Felix. Che belleza! Come la invidio. (*He puts the ice on the table up* LC *and moves back to* c) Buon viaggo, Principesa, e arrividerci.

(Felix *exits up* c)

Verner. What was all that about?

Maud. Nothing much. I just told him I was going back to Rome and he said how he envied me and wished me well. He's a nice boy. We're quite old friends. I knew him first when he was at the Excelsior.

Verner. What shall it be? Scotch, gin, vodka? Or would you like some champagne?

Maud. No, thanks. Vodka would be lovely, with a little tonic and lots of ice. (*She rises*)

(Verner *makes the drink.* Anna-Mary *enters down* L, *moves to* c, *takes Maud by the hand and kisses her*)

Anna-Mary. Why, Maud, isn't this just *wonderful*? I'd no *idea* you were here. When you phoned this morning I couldn't believe it. I had to pinch myself. My! But you look cute as a June-bug with all those gorgeous bangles. Come and sit down right here and tell me all the gossip. (*She pulls Maud round and sits* R *on the sofa*) How's dear Lulu?

Maud (*sitting* L *on the sofa*) I don't know. I haven't seen her for ages. I've been here for the last two weeks staying with my son and his wife.

Anna-Mary. Why, Maud! You take the breath right out of my body! Nobody ever told me you had a son!

Maud. It isn't exactly a topic of universal interest.

Anna-Mary. But how old is he? What does he *do*? Is he handsome? Do you adore him? I've just got to meet him.

Maud. I don't think he's really your cup of tea. He paints abstract pictures and he's a Communist.

Anna-Mary (*shocked to the marrow*) A Communist!

Maud. I don't mean that he's actually a member of the "party", but he's terribly red-minded. He's also going through a grubby phase at the moment. They have a ghastly little flat in Pully and a lot of beatnik cronies. It's all quite fun really.

(VERNER *moves* C *with Maud's drink and his own*)

VERNER. Here's your booze, Princess.
MAUD. Thanks, pal.

(VERNER *sits down* L *with his drink, and lights a cigarette*)

ANNA-MARY. And you say he's got a wife?
MAUD. Yes, she's small and sharp, like a little needle. She used to be a dancer in the Festival ballet and she's just had a baby. That's why I've been here for so long; it sort of hung back. All those "Giselles" and "Swan Lakes" make child-bearing a little complicated.
ANNA-MARY (*offering Maud a cigarette*) And she had the baby?
MAUD. Yes. (*Refusing the cigarette*) No, thank you. Late last night, in the hospital. It's a boy and it weighed exactly what it ought to weigh and was bright red, possibly out of deference to its father's political views. Anyhow, I am now a grandmother, which is a sobering thought.
ANNA-MARY. No one would believe it. You look sensational!
MAUD. So do you, Anna-Mary, so do you. That particular colour is very becoming.
ANNA-MARY. Yes, nice, isn't it.
MAUD. Now I come to think of it, you wore blue that night in Rome when you came to dine.
ANNA-MARY. And how is that *divine* little apartment? I was saying to Clare Pethrington at lunch today that it was just *the* most picturesque place I ever saw, wasn't I, Verner?
VERNER (*laconically*) Yes, sweetheart.
MAUD. Clare hates it. She says there are too many stairs and that it smells of fish. Which is only to be expected really, because there happens to be a fishmonger on the ground floor. I keep on burning incense and dabbing the light bulbs with Miss Dior, but it doesn't do any good.
ANNA-MARY. You know, I'm just heartbroken that you can't come to dinner tonight. It's going to be loads of fun. I've got Mariette and Henri, the Pethringtons of course, Sir Gerard and Lady Nutfield—he was the Governor of somewhere and he looks so British you just want to stand up and sing "God Save the Queen" the moment he comes into the room! Then there are the Carpinchos —they're Brazilian and as cute as they can be—and Bobo Larkin, who's promised to play the piano in the bar afterwards, providing we keep everybody out, and darling old Irma Bidmeyer, who lives in this very hotel and plays bridge with the Queen of Spain— (*Looking out front*) —and last but not least, Their Royal Highnesses!
MAUD. Not Royal, dear, just Serene.

(ANNA-MARY *looks at Maud*)

Anna-Mary (*visibly shaken*) Maud! Is that really true? Are you positive?

Maud. Quite. But you needn't worry about it; it doesn't make any difference. So long as everybody calls him "Sir" and bobs up and down like a cork, he's as happy as a clam.

Anna-Mary. But I could have *sworn* that Mariette said . . .

Maud (*laughing*) Mariette's terribly vague about that sort of thing. She once lost her head at an official reception in Geneva and addressed poor old Prince Paniowtovski as "Ma'am". She wasn't far out at that.

Verner (*with a guffaw*) You know that's funny! That's very funny!

Anna-Mary (*ignoring this*) Do you mean I have to *introduce* him as His Serene Highness?

Maud. You don't have to introduce him at all. You just take people up to him and say: "Sir—may I present So-and-so." He may buck a bit at Irma Bidmeyer—he's notoriously anti-Semitic—but you can always mumble.

Verner. Well—what do you know?

Anna-Mary (*crossly*) Do be quiet, Verner, and stop interrupting.

Verner. Okay, sweetheart.

Anna-Mary. Why don't you make yourself useful for once and go down to the bar and ask if they've got any of those cigars. I want to have a little private visit with Maud.

Verner (*rising and moving* c) Okay, sweetheart.

Anna-Mary. And for heaven's sake take those golf-clubs with you.

(Verner *picks up the golf-clubs*)

Maud. Oh, don't send him away. I've hardly talked to him at all.

Verner. Don't worry, Princess. I'll just set the table, fix the flowers, give a hundred dollars to each of the waiters and be right back.

(Verner *exits up* c. Anna-Mary *rises, moves up* c *and closes the door behind him, then returns down* c *before speaking*)

Anna-Mary. Verner really gets on my nerves sometimes.

Maud (*quizzically*) Yes. I see he does.

Anna-Mary. He's just plain stubborn. He refuses to be interested in any of the things I'm interested in, he doesn't like any of the people I like.

Maud. He doesn't seem to mind me.

Anna-Mary (*sitting in the* c *chair*) Only because you lay yourself out to be nice to him.

Maud. Perhaps that's what he needs.

Anna-Mary. You were just darling to him that night we dined with you. I remember saying to Lulu afterwards, Maud's just wonderful, she's warm, she's human, and what's more, she's a giver and not a taker.

Maud. You mustn't overrate me, Anna-Mary. I'm a taker all right when I get the chance.

Anna-Mary (*rising and taking the cigarette-box from the* c *table to offer to Maud*) Why, Maud Caragnani, that's just plain nonsense and you know it!

(Maud *refuses a cigarette.* Anna-Mary *returns to her seat and takes out one for herself*)

You can't fool me! The one thing I flatter myself I'm never wrong about is people. Why do you suppose it is that you're so popular? That everybody's always running after you and asking you everywhere?

Maud. It's very sweet of you to say so, but I'm afraid you exaggerate my social graces.

Anna-Mary. I'm not talking about social graces, honey. I'm talking about "character" and "heart"! You're just basically "sympathique" and there's no getting away from it. And above all you go through life *making an effort!* Now, Verner just will not make an effort. He just stands around waiting for people to come to him, instead of him going to them. Do you see what I mean? (*She lights her cigarette*)

Maud. Perfectly. But I find it difficult to believe that he could have made the enormous fortune he has if he were all that lacka-daisical.

Anna-Mary. Oh, he's sharp enough in business, I'll grant you that, but he just won't open his eyes to *experience*. I mean he deliberately shuts his eyes to the *beauty* of things. You'd never credit it, but in the whole five months we've been in Europe this trip he's only been inside three churches!

Maud (*laughing*) Perhaps he doesn't like churches.

Anna-Mary. I managed to drag him into Saint Peter's in Rome and all he did was stomp around humming "I like New York in June" under his breath. I was mortified.

Maud. Oh, poor Buffalo Bill!

Anna-Mary. What on *earth* do you mean by that?

Maud. It's how I see Verner in my mind's eye. A sort of frustrated Buffalo Bill who's had his horse taken away from him.

Anna-Mary (*snappily*) Verner can't ride horseback.

Maud. There's still time for him to learn.

Anna-Mary. He's turned fifty-five. His arteries wouldn't stand it.

Maud. There are different sorts of horses. Pegasus, for instance. He had wings.

Anna-Mary. You know something, Maud? I haven't the faintest idea what you're talking about.

(*The telephone rings. Anna-Mary rises to answer it*)

Maud.   Verner. We're both talking about Verner. But from different points of view.

Anna-Mary (*answering the telephone,* l *of the table*) Hallo? . . . Yes, speaking . . . Bobo! My dear, I never recognized your voice. . . . What! You can't mean it—you can't be serious! . . . But when did it happen? I mean, you sounded perfectly all right on the phone this morning . . . Oh, my God . . . (*There is an anguished pause while she listens*) But, Bobo, you can't do this to me, at the very last minute. I just can't stand it . . . (*She moves to* c, *carrying the phone*) But if you don't come we shall be thirteen at table . . . But, Bobo honey, I was *counting* on you! I've made all the arrangements about the piano in the bar after dinner and everything . . . Well, all I can say is that it's just disaster, that's all, absolute disaster . . . Couldn't you just manage to come for the dinner? That would be better than nothing . . . A hundred and two! Are you *sure* it's a hundred and two? When did you take it? . . . What—the doctor says you're not to talk any more on the phone? But, Bobo . . . (*She closes her eyes in despair and replaces the receiver*) He hung up on me. He just hung up on me! (*She puts the phone back on the table*) After dealing me the worst blow in my life, he has the nerve to hang up on me. (*Moving* l) I'll never speak to that god-damned little pansy again as long as there's breath left in my body.

Maud. Be reasonable, Anna-Mary. You can't expect the poor devil to come to dinner if he's got a temperature of a hundred and two.

Anna-Mary. Reasonable! Seven o'clock, thirteen at table, and you ask me to be reasonable!

Maud. Can you think of anyone else?

Anna-Mary. Of course I can't. We only got here last night. You'll have to come, Maud, you'll just *have* to. It'll make one woman too many, but that can't be helped.

Maud. I really can't possibly. I haven't even got an evening dress with me, and I have to drive to Rome.

Anna-Mary. Oh, Maud, go to Rome later, go to Rome any time, but just help me out tonight. (*She moves* c) You don't have to worry about an evening dress. I can lend you a divine Balenciaga model (*moving down* l) I've only worn twice. Oh, Maud—for heaven's sake —I don't know where I'm at. This is a ghastly situation. I think I'm going crazy.

Maud. Why don't you ring up Mariette? She might have somebody on tap for just this sort of crisis.

Anna-Mary (*moving to* l *of the sofa and kneeling*) You really won't come? I'd bless you until my dying day if only you would.

MAUD (*shaking her head*) It's quite out of the question.

ANNA-MARY. You mean you don't *want* to come.

MAUD. To be perfectly frank, I don't. (*Rising to between the chairs* L) In the first place I haven't spoken to either of the Pethringtons for three years . . .

(ANNA-MARY *rises to* R *of Maud*)

I can't stand the sight of dear old Irma Bidmeyer, and I think the Prince is the most lascivious, vulgar old bore it has ever been my misfortune to meet.

ANNA-MARY (*outraged at such lèse-majesté*) Maud!

MAUD. But leaving all else aside, I've promised to pick up my son at the hospital and take him off to dine at the Grappe d'Or. They probably won't let him in if he looks anything like he looked earlier in the day, but it's the last chance I shall have of seeing him for a long time. Why don't you call up Mariette as I suggested?

ANNA-MARY (*going to the telephone*) This is ghastly—just ghastly!

MAUD. Don't take it so hard, Anna-Mary. I'm quite sure the Prince would waive the most atavistic superstition for the sake of a free meal. (*She sits in the* C *chair*)

ANNA-MARY. I just don't know how you can sit there, Maud, and say such terrible things.

MAUD. We just happen to be talking about the same person from different points of view again, don't we? Only in this case I happen to know him and you don't.

ANNA-MARY (*lifting the receiver*) Operator—Operator—Operator —donnez-moi— (*She glances at the telephone pad*) —donnez-moi— vingt-trois—trente-six—vingt-deux s'il vous plait et aussi vite que possible on account of je suis presse. (*She moves* C *with the telephone. Balefully, to Maud*) The next time I see that Bobo Larkin I'll just make him wish he'd never been born.

MAUD. He's probably wishing that at this very moment if he's got a temperature of a hundred and two.

ANNA-MARY (*into the receiver*) 'Allo—'Allo—ici Mrs Conklin. Je veux parler avec le comtesse, s'il vous plait . . . What? I mean comment? . . . Je ne comprends pas—parlez vous Anglais. (*To Maud*) It's a different man from the one I talked to before.

(MAUD *rises to take the telephone*)

I can't understand a word he's saying.

MAUD. Give it to me. (*She takes the telephone*)

(ANNA-MARY *moves* L *of Maud*)

'Allo—c'est de la part de Madame Conklin, est-ce que Madame la comtesse est la? . . . Oui . . . Elle est sortie? . . . Depuis quand? . . . Vous savez ou? . . . Oui, jecoute, un cocktail chez Madame de

Vosanges. Oui. Vous ne savez pas le numero par hazard? . . . Ah bon, je vais le chercher. Merci beaucoup. (*She hangs up*) She left ten minutes ago to go to a cocktail-party and she's not coming back before dinner.

ANNA-MARY. I think I'm going out of my mind. (*She sits* C)

MAUD (*replacing the telephone*) Somebody called Vosanges. I don't know them, but they're sure to be in the book. (*She looks up the number in the directory above the sofa*)

(VERNER *enters up* C, *with a box of cigars*)

VERNER. What's cooking?

ANNA-MARY. The most terrible thing's happened.

MAUD. Bobo Larkin's get a temperature of a hundred and two.

VERNER. Well—what do you know? Who the hell's Bobo Larkin?

ANNA-MARY (*with dreadful patience*) It doesn't matter *who* he is, Verner. But what does matter is *where* he is. And *where* he is is in bed with a fever, which means that he can't come to dinner, nor can he play the piano in the bar *after* dinner.

VERNER (*moving down* C) Poor guy. (*Giving Anna-Mary the cigars*) Probably a virus of some sort.

ANNA-MARY. It can be a virus or bubonic plague for all I care, but what it means is that we shall be thirteen at table.

VERNER. Well—well—well. (*Looking at Maud*) Boy, are we in trouble? (*He laughs*)

ANNA-MARY (*icily*) There's nothing to laugh about, Verner. It'll *ruin* the whole evening.

VERNER. Sorry, sweetheart. It's just nerves. (*He moves down* L *and sits. To Maud*) What about you, Princess? How about you pinch-hitting for this Bozo what's his name? (*He lights a cigarette*)

MAUD. Not even for you, Verner. Also I can't play the piano, in the bar or anywhere else. I've found the number, Anna-Mary. Do you want me to ring it and see if I can get hold of Mariette?

ANNA-MARY (*rising, putting the cigars on the table down* L *and returning to above Verner*) No, it's too late. And anyway I couldn't have her just dragging *anyone* along to meet Royalty. There's only one thing to be done. Verner—you must have your dinner up here.

VERNER. Huh?

MAUD (*sitting on the* L *arm of the sofa*) Won't that seem a little odd?

ANNA-MARY. It can't be helped. We'll pretend you're sick or something.

VERNER. You can say I've got a temperature of a hundred and three!

ANNA-MARY. You *could* be waiting for an important business call from New York.

MAUD. No, Anna-Mary. That would be *lèse-majesté*.

VERNER. You could always say I've got a galloping hernia.

ANNA-MARY (*losing her temper*) You think this is very funny, don't you? (*Moving* C) Both you and Maud? Well, all I can say is I'm very sorry I can't share the joke. Mariette's been just wonderful, making arrangements for this dinner for me tonight. We've been phoning each other back and forth for weeks. She's the only one who has taken the trouble to plan it all for *my* sake, and if only for *her* sake I'm going to see that it's a success if it's the last thing I do. And I'd like to say one thing more, because I just can't keep it in any longer. I'm bitterly disappointed in you, Maud, and it's no use pretending I'm not. I think it's real mean of you not to stand by me tonight and help me out of this jam. You could perfectly easily come to dinner if you wanted to.

MAUD (*calmly*) Certainly I could, but, as I have already explained to you, I don't want to, and, as you may remember, I also said why.

ANNA-MARY. I can remember that you were insulting about my guests and said the Prince was vulgar, and I just don't happen to think that's a nice way to talk.

VERNER. Listen, sweetheart, let's not have a brawl, shall we?

ANNA-MARY (*ignoring him, to Maud*) You've hurt me, Maud, more than I can say. You've let me down. And I thought you were a friend.

MAUD (*coldly*) Why?

VERNER. Holy mackerel!

MAUD (*inexorably, to Anna-Mary*) We have met casually three or four times and you have dined with me once. Is that, according to your curious behaviour, sufficient basis for a lifelong affection?

ANNA-MARY (*with grandeur*) I do not give my friendship as easily as you seem to think, Maud, and when I do it is only to those who are truly sincere and willing to stand by me in time of trouble. After all, that is what friendship is for, isn't it? It's a question of give and take. However, I do not wish to discuss the matter any further. I am sorry that there should have been this little misunderstanding between us, and I can only hope that the next time our paths cross the clouds will have rolled away and everything will be forgiven and forgotten. If you will excuse me now I must go and dress and do my hair. (*She moves below the* C *chair to Verner*) Verner, you will have your dinner up here, and can ring for the waiter and order it whenever you feel like it. And I'd be very glad if you would ring down to the Maitre D and tell him I'll be in the dining-room at eight o'clock to rearrange the place cards.

(ANNA-MARY *bows coldly to Maud and exits down* L)

MAUD (*after a pause*) Well, that's that, isn't it?

VERNER. She sure is good and mad.

MAUD. Oh, I'm sorry. I'm afraid it's partly my fault. I was rather beastly to her.

VERNER. Forget it. Anna-Mary's tough. She can take it.

Maud. Yes, I'm sure she can. But I hate being beastly to people. It's only that she made me suddenly angry. I wish I hadn't been.

Verner (*rising, taking his own glass, and Maud's from the* c *table, and moving to the drinks table*) Have another drink.

Maud (*rising*) No, thank you. I really must go now.

Verner. Come on, just a small one.

Maud (*glancing at her watch*) Very well, but make it a really small one. I must leave at a quarter past.

Verner. Atta girl! (*He pours drinks as before*)

Maud (*sitting* r *on the sofa*) What an idiotic little drama. (*She sighs*) Oh dear!

Verner. Snap out of it, Princess. It ain't worth worrying about. Anna-Mary always raises hell when things don't happen to go just the way she wants.

Maud. Yes, I expect she does.

Verner. I don't pay no mind to it any more.

Maud. Are you disappointed? About being forbidden to go to your own dinner-party, I mean?

Verner (*moving down* c *with the drinks*) It's just about breaking my heart. (*He gives Maud her drink and sits* l *of her*)

Maud (*with a smile*) Yes. I suspect it is. (*She raises her glass to him*) Well, here's to the next time we meet. When all those clouds have rolled away and everything is forgiven and forgotten.

Verner (*raising his glass*) Here's to the next time we meet anyway, whether everything's been forgiven and forgotten or not.

Maud. Thank you, Verner. I'll remember that.

Verner. Do you want to know something?

Maud. Shoot, pal.

Verner. That evening we had with you in Rome was the high-spot of our whole trip—for me.

Maud. Only because I "laid myself out to be nice to you". That's what Anna-Mary told me earlier on this evening.

Verner. Well, Momma was dead on the nose for once. You sure did.

Maud. And it worked, apparently.

Verner. Princess, it worked like a charm.

Maud. Would you mind if I asked you a very personal question, almost an impertinent one, as a matter of fact?

Verner. Go right ahead.

Maud. You really are a very rich man, aren't you?

Verner. If that's the question, I guess the answer's yes.

Maud. It isn't. The question is more complicated than that, and I wouldn't even ask it if I didn't like you enough to be genuinely interested. (*She pauses*)

Verner (*sipping his drink and looking at her*) Well?

Maud. Why, when you can easily afford to do whatever you like, do you allow yourself to be continually bullied into doing what you don't like?

VERNER.   That sure is a sixty-four-thousand-dollar question all right.

MAUD. You must have asked it to yourself occasionally. You're nobody's fool.

VERNER (*looking down*) Maybe I have, Princess. Maybe I have.

MAUD. And did you give yourself the sixty-four-thousand-dollar answer?

VERNER (*rising and moving* c) No, Princess. I guess I goofed it.

MAUD. Yes, dear Buffalo Bill. I'm sadly afraid you did.

VERNER (*putting his glass on the* c *table*) Hey! What's this Buffalo Bill bit?

MAUD. Just one of my little personal fancies. I puzzled Anna-Mary with it a short while ago. I said you needed a horse.

VERNER. A horse? Are you out of your mind? What the hell should I do with a horse?

MAUD (*laughing*) Jump on its back and gallop away on it. Failing a horse, a dolphin would be better than nothing. There was a little boy in Greek mythology, I believe, who had an excellent seat on a dolphin. It took him skimming along over the blue waves of the Aegean, and he never had to go to any dinner-parties or meet any important people, and whenever they came to rest on a rock or a little white beach, the dolphin would dive deep, deep down and bring him up a golden fish. It's high time somebody gave you a golden fish, Verner. It would mean nothing on the Stock Exchange, but it might light up your whole sad world.

VERNER (*astonished*) Well, I'll be god-damned!

MAUD (*rising purposefully to* c) I must go now. I promised my son I'd be at the hospital at seven-thirty.

VERNER (*with feeling*) Don't go yet, Princess. Please stay.

MAUD. I can't. I really can't. But we'll meet again. (*She collects her bag from the desk, then returns to Verner*) Good-bye for the moment, dear Buffalo Bill. Don't forget me too soon. (*She kisses him unexpectedly on the cheek*)

MAUD *runs out up* c *and* VERNER *sinks into the* c *chair as the* LIGHTS *fade to* BLACK-OUT *and—*

the CURTAIN *falls*

Scene 2

Scene—*The same. Several hours have passed and it is now about eleven o'clock in the evening.*

When the Curtain *rises and* Lights *fade up,* Verner *is lying stretched out on the sofa reading a James Bond novel. He has taken off his tie and his shirt is open at the neck. There is a trolley* R *with the remains of his dinner on it.*

There is a discreet knock on the door.

Verner. Come in—entrez.

(Felix *enters up* c *with a bottle of Evian water in a large bucket of ice on a tray*)

Felix. I hope I do not intrude, Monsieur, but Madame requested a bottle of Evian bien glacée to be put by her bed.
Verner. Okay. Go right ahead.

(Felix *exits down* l *with the tray, then re-enters up to* c)

Felix. I regret not having taken away the table before, Monsieur, but I am single-handed on this floor tonight and there has been much to do.
Verner. Don't worry, that's all right with me.
Felix. Monsieur has need of anything?
Verner (*thoughtfully*) Yeah—it seems that I have. I have need of a golden fish.
Felix. Pardon, Monsieur?
Verner. Never mind. Skip it. Give me a bourbon on the rocks.
Felix. Bien, Monsieur. (*He pours a bourbon on ice*)
Verner (*sitting up* l *of the sofa*) Princess Caragnani said she knew you before. In Rome, wasn't it?
Felix. Yes, sir. I served in the bar at the Excelsior for several months. Only as third barman, though. The Princess often was there with friends.
Verner. She has a lot of friends in Rome, hasn't she?
Felix (*with enthusiasm*) Ah si, Signore, e una donna molta incantevole, tutto il mondo . . .
Verner. Hey, none of that; stick to English.
Felix. I was saying that she is a lady much enchanted and that all the world are most fond of her.
Verner (*a little wistfully*) Yeah—I'll bet they are.
Felix (*bringing Verner the drink on a tray*) Your drink, Monsieur.
Verner. Thanks. (*He takes it*) Molto gratzie!

Felix (*delighted*) Ah, bravo! Il signore cominca imparare l'Italiano! Monsieur is beginning to learn my language.

Verner. I guess it's never too late to try—to try to learn someone else's language.

Felix. It is difficult at first, but here in La Suisse there is much opportunity because there are so many languages spoken.

Verner (*with a little laugh*) You're telling me! Have you got a girl?

Felix. Oh yes, Monsieur.

Verner. Is she here in Lausanne?

Felix. No, Signore. She is in Italy.

Verner. What's her name?

Felix. Renata.

Verner. Are you crazy about her?

Felix. No, Signore. But we are most fond. I have taught her to water-ski.

Verner. Are you going to marry her?

Felix (*with a slight shrug*) Che sa? One day, perhaps, but first I must make the money to afford it.

Verner. Can you ride horseback?

Felix (*puzzled*) No, Signore. But in the village where I was born my uncle had a mule which I used to ride in the mountains. Era un animale molto cattivo. It was a most angry animal.

Verner. And a dolphin—did you ever try a dolphin, when you were a kid?

Felix. I fear I do not understand.

Verner. You know, a porpoise—a kinda fish . . . (*He makes a gesture illustrating a porpoise jumping*)

(Felix *looks at him in some dismay*)

Felix. Ah si—un porco marino—un delfino! Monsieur makes the little joke?

Verner. Yeah. I guess you're right. It was only a little joke.

Felix. Is there anything more that Monsieur requires?

Verner. Yeah, Felix. I'm beginning to think there is. You can take away the table now.

Felix (*moving the trolley to* c *and opening the doors*) Bien, Monsieur.

Verner (*taking out a fifty-dollar bill*) Here. Buy a present for Renata.

(Felix *takes the bill and starts to move away, then looks at it and returns*)

Felix. Monsieur has made a mistake. This is fifty dollars.

Verner. No, Felix. It ain't no mistake. I guess the only thing that Monsieur never makes a mistake about is money. Have yourself a ball. Good night, Felix.

Felix (*overwhelmed*) Mile mille grazie, Signore. Monsieur is most generous. (*He pockets the bill and moves to the doors*) A domani, Signore, a dormani.

(Felix *bows and exits up* c *with the dinner trolley.* Verner, *left alone, returns to his book, tries to read it for a moment or two, then flings it down. He is about to light a cigarette when the telephone rings. He rises and moves above the sofa to answer it*)

Verner. Hallo? . . . Yes, speaking. (*His voice lightens*) Oh, it's you! Where are you? . . . Here, in the lobby? . . . Yeah, come up—come right on up. (*He replaces the telephone then stares at it for a moment with a beaming smile. Then he runs to the mirror up* l *and puts on his tie, empties the ashtrays from the occasional tables into the basket up* l, *puts on his jacket, straightens the sofa cushions, moves to* c, *and waits. Suddenly he realizes he has no shoes on. He runs to the sofa, sits* c, *and puts them on. Then he returns to* c *and waits again*)

(*There is a knock on the door* c. Verner *opens it.* Maud *enters*)

Maud. Hallo, Buffalo Bill. How was your lonely bivouac?
Verner (*grinning with pleasure*) Hi!
Maud. I'm sure you say that to every taxi you see.
Verner. Come right in, Princess. (*He takes her coat and puts it over the desk chair*) Come right in and put your feet up.
Maud (*putting her bag on the desk and sitting* l *on the sofa*) I think it would be more discreet to leave them down.
Verner (*closing the doors and coming down* c) This is great! Just great! I nearly flipped when I heard your voice on the phone just now. I didn't think I was going to see you again for quite a while.
Maud. No. Neither did I. It seemed a pity.
Verner. I'd just been talking about you, only a few minutes ago . . .
Maud. Talking about me? Who to?
Verner. Felix, the waiter. He's just crazy about you.
Maud. Is he indeed?
Verner. He said that you were a lady much enchanted.
Maud. Italians have a flair for romantic exaggeration. Aren't you going to offer me a drink?
Verner. You bet. What'll it be?
Maud. Brandy, I think, only very little. I have a long drive ahead of me.
Verner (*moving to the drinks table and pouring one neat brandy*) You really are going to drive all through the night?
Maud. Yes. I'm looking forward to it. There's a moon and there's not much snow left on the pass; the road will be fairly clear.
Verner. Do you want anything with the brandy? Soda or water or ice?

MAUD. No, nothing, thanks, just neat. (*A slight pause*) Why were you talking about me to Felix?

VERNER (*bringing down her glass*) I don't know. You said you'd known him in Rome.

MAUD (*taking the glass*) I see.

VERNER. And I guess you were on my mind.

MAUD. You were on my mind, too. I talked about you to my son at dinner.

VERNER. What did you say?

MAUD. I can't remember. Nothing very much. Just that I liked you.

VERNER. And what did *he* say?

MAUD. He asked me how long it was before babies started to talk. I replied that in some cases it took a lifetime. (*She laughs*)

VERNER. Why are you laughing?

MAUD. It's been quite a funny evening one way and another. He's in a state of blissful euphoria. The fact of becoming a father has completely transformed him. He had his beard shaved off this afternoon, and his hair cut. He even put on a coat and tie for dinner. He had a bottle of champagne and he babbled away like a brook.

VERNER (*moving down* R *below the sofa*) Are you very close, you and your son? (*He offers her a cigarette*)

MAUD (*refusing*) Not really. But we seemed to be tonight. I don't much care for his wife and I think he knows it. She's actually not a bad little thing *au fond*, but she's a bit neurotic.

VERNER. What's his name? Your son, I mean?

MAUD. Faber. His father's name was Fabrizio, and Faber was the nearest I could get to it in English.

VERNER. This Fabrizio—what was he like?

MAUD. Handsome, vain, charming and badly mother-ridden. She was an old devil and hated me like the plague. I rather see her point now. Being a mother-in-law isn't all jam.

VERNER. Were you in love with him?

MAUD. Oh yes. But it didn't last long. We'd only been married for a year when he was killed in a car crash. That was in 1940. I managed to get myself on to a ship going to Lisbon, and from there back to England. Faber was born in Cornwall.

VERNER (*moving to down* L) Did you ever see any of them again?

MAUD. Oh yes. After the war was over I came back to Italy to live. I made the old girl fork out enough money to pay for Faber's education. In the last years of her life we almost became friends.

VERNER (*after a pause*) Why did you come back to see me tonight?

MAUD. A sudden impulse. I was on my way to Pully to pick up my suitcase from Faber's flat and I was driving along, just out there by the lake, and I thought of you sitting up here all by yourself, so I turned the car round and came back. I thought you might be lonely.

VERNER. That was mighty kind of you, Princess. (*He looks at her intently*) I was. (*He sits* C)

MAUD. Aren't you going to have a drink? To keep me company?

VERNER. Yes, in a minute, after I've asked you a sixty-four-thousand-dollar question.

MAUD. Shoot, pal!

VERNER. Why did you kiss me like you did when you went away before dinner?

MAUD. Another sudden impulse. I'm a very impulsive character. It's often got me into trouble.

VERNER. And you came back because you thought I might be lonesome?

MAUD. Yes. That was one of the reasons.

VERNER. There were others?

MAUD. Yes.

VERNER. What were they?

MAUD. They're difficult to put into words. You have to be a master psychologist to dissect an emotional impulse successfully. Just as you have to be an expert watchmaker to be able to take a watch to pieces and put it together again. I'm not an expert in either of those fields. I'm afraid of being clumsy and making a botch of it.

VERNER. I don't reckon you could ever be clumsy.

MAUD (*with a slight smile*) Thank you, Verner. Let's hope your reckoning is accurate.

VERNER. You said "emotional impulse". Was that right?

MAUD. Yes. Up to a point.

VERNER. Do you class "pity" as an emotion?

MAUD. Yes. But it was more than pity that made me turn the car round.

VERNER (*putting out his cigarette*) That's what I was aiming to find out.

MAUD. Well, now that you've found out, you can get yourself a drink and let me out of the witness-box.

VERNER (*rising*) Okay, lady. You're the boss. (*He goes to the drinks table and pours himself a bourbon and ice*)

MAUD. That remark is sadly significant.

VERNER. How come?

MAUD. I've never been to America.

VERNER. It's a great country.

MAUD (*thoughtfully*) I suppose American men must like being bossed by their women, otherwise they wouldn't put up with it.

VERNER (*moving down* LC *with his glass. A little defensive*) You can't judge Americans by the ones you meet in Europe.

MAUD. I've heard that said before. I'm not quite sure that I believe it. After all, the English and French and Italians seem to retain their basic characteristics wherever they are. I can't see why it should be only the Americans who are geographically unstable.

VERNER. You know, Princess, you sure do say the damnedest things.

MAUD (*repentant*) I know I do. That's what I meant just now by being clumsy. Please forgive me.

VERNER. There ain't nothing to forgive.

MAUD. I really came back to be a comfort, not an irritant.

VERNER (*looking at her intently*) The fact that you came back at all is good enough for me.

MAUD (*meeting his eye*) Is it, Verner? Is it really?

VERNER. You know damn well it is. (*He takes her glass, puts both it and his own on the table* C, *then lifts her gently to her feet, puts his arms round her and presses his mouth on to hers*)

(*They stand quite still for a few moments, locked in their embrace, then* MAUD *draws away*)

MAUD. I knew perfectly well that that was going to happen, and yet somehow it was a surprise.

VERNER (*a little huskily*) I guess I knew, too. But I wasn't quite sure, and I reckon I was a bit scared.

MAUD. Scared?

VERNER. Scared that you'd give me the brush-off, or laugh at me.

MAUD. Why should I laugh at you?

VERNER. I don't mean that I really thought you would, you're too kind to do that, but—well—I'm not the sort of guy who likes to kid himself.

MAUD (*gently*) No. I don't think you are.

VERNER. I mean, I've seen too many fellers of my age suddenly go berserk and get themselves into trouble, bad trouble.

MAUD. Would you describe that kiss you gave me just now as going berserk?

VERNER (*ruefully*) Now you *are* laughing at me.

MAUD. These fellows of your own age you talk about. How old are they?

VERNER (*grinning*) Old enough to know better.

MAUD. And this trouble their sudden madness gets them into, this bad trouble—what does it consist of?

VERNER (*making and anti-clockwise circle round downstage and back to her*) Oh, all kinds of things, making fools of themselves, getting in wrong with everyone, waking up one fine morning and realizing that they've been played for a sucker.

MAUD. Do you consider, off hand, that I'm playing you for a sucker?

Verner (*hurriedly*) No, Princess, you know damn well I don't—I didn't mean that at all.

Maud. How old are you, anyhow?

Verner. Fifty-five, pushing fifty-six.

Maud. Well, I'm forty-four and a grandmother. I'm ashamed of you, Buffalo Bill, running around making passes at grandmothers.

Verner (*worried*) What are we going to do?

Maud. What are we going to do about what?

Verner. About this! About us?

Maud (*putting her arms round his neck*) We could always go berserk again.

(*They go into another long embrace*)

Verner. You're sensational—d'you know that? You're just sensational.

Maud. I believe you really mean it.

Verner. Mean it! I'm crazy about you! (*He moves towards her*)

Maud (*backing away*) No, really—Verner, dear Verner, this has gone far enough. We're both behaving very foolishly . . .

Verner. What's so foolish about it?

Maud. It's my own fault, I know. I should never have let it get to this point.

Verner. Why?

Maud (*sitting* R *on the sofa*) Because nothing can come of it; there's no sense in us allowing ourselves to get emotionally involved with each other. There's too much in the way. You know that as well as I do.

Verner. I don't know any such thing. All I know is I've fallen in love with you, and all I *want* to know is whether you've fallen in love with me. It's as simple as that. Once that's clear, all the other complications can be taken care of. Have you? (*He sits* L *on the sofa*) Or rather, could you—do you think—be in love with me?

Maud (*looking at him*) Yes, Verner. I think I could and I think I am. Falling in love sounds so comprehensive and all-embracing and violent. It's the stuff of youth, really, not of middle age, and yet—and yet . . .

Verner (*urgently*) And yet—what?

Maud (*genuinely moved, rising to below the* C *chair*) I don't know. I'm feeling suddenly conscience-stricken.

Verner. About Anna-Mary?

Maud. No, not about Anna-Mary. You said yourself earlier this evening that she was tough and could take it. You're dead right; she's as tough as old boots. If any woman in the world asked for this situation to happen to her, she did. I have no conscience whatsoever about Anna-Mary. But you—it's you I'm worrying about.

Verner. Why?

MAUD (*kneeling by the L arm of the sofa*) I wouldn't like you to get hurt. As a matter of fact, I'm not any too anxious to get hurt myself.

VERNER. There's no fun in gambling on certainties.

MAUD. What exactly do you want of me? Have you thought?

VERNER. No. I haven't had time to think. I only know I want you.

MAUD (*rising to below the c chair*) You don't know me really at all. You don't know anything about me.

VERNER. So what? Come to that, you don't know so much about me.

MAUD. I think I know enough.

VERNER. That goes for me, too.

MAUD. It's not quite so simple as that. We've lived in completely separate worlds, you and I. The standards and codes of behaviour and moral values on this side of the Atlantic aren't the same as those you've been brought up to believe in. I'm not saying that they're either better or worse, but they are profoundly different.

VERNER. It seems to me that people are much the same all the world over, once you get below the surface.

MAUD (*sitting on the L arm of the sofa with her arm round Verner*) That, darling Buffalo Bill, is a platitude, and an inaccurate one at that. People are *not* the same all the world over. When you get below the surface of an American you can still find a quality of innocence. There is no innocence left in Europe.

VERNER. What are you trying to say?

MAUD. I'm trying to warn you, really. I could never have lived the sort of life I've lived, in your country. It wouldn't have been possible.

VERNER. How do you mean—the sort of life you've lived? You're scaring the hell out of me.

MAUD (*with a slight laugh*) Oh, it hasn't been as bad as all that, but I am, I suppose, what the old-fashioned novelists would describe as "A Woman With a Past".

VERNER (*dryly*) I hate to have to admit it, Princess, but we have had just one or two of those in the United States.

MAUD. Oh, I know—I know. But it still isn't quite the same thing. (*She pauses*)

VERNER. Okay—okay—let's let it go at that.

MAUD. Nor do I wish to give you the impression that my life has been one long promiscuous orgy.

VERNER. Bully for you, Princess.

MAUD (*determined to be honest*) But I have had lovers—here and there along the line.

VERNER. If you'd been in America, they'd have been husbands and you could have soaked them for alimony and been a damn sight better off.

Maud. Oh, Verner! You really are very sweet. (*She kisses him, then slides over the arm of the sofa to sit beside him*)

Verner (*holding her*) C'mon, what's all this about?

Maud. I just don't want you to be disillusioned.

Verner. That'll be the day.

Maud. I don't want you to wake up one morning like those other fellows, those other romantic innocents, and find that you've been played for a sucker.

Verner (*shaking her gently*) Once and for all will you lay off that kind of talk!

Maud. Okay, pal. I was only trying to be honest.

Verner (*letting her go*) And get it into your head that it ain't your past I'm interested in, but your future. And that includes me. Do I make myself clear?

Maud (*looking down*) Yes, Verner. Quite clear.

Verner. Well, that being settled, where do we go from here?

Maud (*suddenly laughing*) What about Rome? It's as good a jumping-off place as anywhere!

Verner. Whatever you say, Princess.

Maud. When will you come? This week? Next month? When?

Verner. This week next month my foot! I'm coming with you tonight!

Maud (*rising*) Verner!

Verner. In that god-damned Volkswagen.

Maud. It's very small and your legs are so long. I'm afraid you'll be miserably uncomfortable.

Verner. The seats slide back, don't they?

Maud. Yes. I'm sure they do . . . (*She breaks off and looks at him*) Oh, Verner, do you really mean this?

Verner. You bet I mean it. What time do we start?

Maud (*suddenly turning away to below the c chair*) I can't let you do this, Verner, I really can't. It's—it's too sudden. You must give yourself time to think . . .

Verner. Are you chickening out on the deal?

Maud. No. It isn't that, really it isn't. I'm thinking of you, not of myself. I meant what I said just now. You haven't any idea what I'm really like. All you know for certain is that I married a Sicilian, had a son in Cornwall and a grandson in Lausanne.

Verner. I know what Felix said.

Maud (*almost crossly*) Did you consult the nearest floor waiter before you took on Anna-Mary?

Verner (*dryly*) Maybe it would have been better if I had. (*He rises to c*)

Maud (*bursting out laughing*) Oh, darling Buffalo Bill, this is ridiculous, it really is.

(VERNER *rises to* C. *They embrace*)

Everything's got out of hand.

VERNER. Now see here, Princess. It was you who went on about the horse and the dolphin and the golden fish. How can I get the golden fish if I'm scared of taking the ride?

MAUD. But you must have loved Anna-Mary once—in the very beginning, I mean?

VERNER. I guess I kidded myself that I did, but not for long. (*He moves below the sofa*) She got me on the rebound, anyway.

MAUD. The rebound?

VERNER. I was married before, to a girl I was crazy about. (*He pauses*) Then, just after Pearl Harbour, when I'd been drafted into the Navy, she got stuck on another guy and went off with him to Mexico. The divorce was fixed up while I was in the Pacific. When I get home to Minneapolis in nineteen forty-six my old man died and I took over the business. (*He sits on the* L *arm of the sofa*) Anna-Mary was there, waiting to greet the conquering hero. I'd known her since she was a kid.

MAUD. Was she pretty?

VERNER. Yeah. That's just about what she was, pretty. Her mother and my mother had been in school together. Everybody put their shoulders to the wheel—it was a natural. We got married and lived happily ever after for all of seven months. There was a good deal of dough around even in those days. Then she got pregnant and had herself an abortion without telling me. I'd wanted a kid more than anything, so it was a kind of disappointment. She pretended at the time that it was a miscarriage, but I found out the truth later.

MAUD (*moving* C) What did she do that for?

VERNER. I don't know. She was scared, I guess. Also she didn't want to spoil her figure. She was always mighty concerned about her figure. I reckon Anna-Mary's eaten enough lettuce in her life to keep a million rabbits happy for a hundred years.

MAUD (*moving down* L) Oh, Verner! What a dismal waste of time.

VERNER. You can say that again.

MAUD. And it never occurred to you to break away?

VERNER. Oh yes. It occurred to me once or twice, but it never seemed worth the trouble. We've led our own lives, Anna-Mary and me. She's had her social junketings and I've had my work, and a couple of little flutters on the side every now and again.

MAUD. Well, I'm glad to hear of that, anyhow.

VERNER. We might have jogged along all right indefinitely if we hadn't started taking these trips to Europe. (*He rises*) Europe plays all hell with women like Anna-Mary; it gives 'em the wrong kind of ambitions.

Maud (*moving to Verner*) I belong to Europe, Verner. I'm European from the top of my head to the soles of my feet. That's why I said just now that you ought to give yourself time to think—before you burn your boats.

Verner. My boats wouldn't burn, honey; they're right down on the waterline anyways. What time do we leave?

Maud (*glancing at her watch*) It's now twenty to twelve. I've got to pick up my suitcase at Faber's flat.

Verner. I'll pack a few things and meet you in the lobby downstairs at twelve-thirty. The rest of my stuff can be sent on.

Maud. You're sure? You're absolutely dead sure?

Verner. Just as sure as I've ever been of anything in my whole life.

Maud. Oh, Verner!

(Verner *takes her in his arms*)

Verner. As soon as I can get a divorce fixed up, we'll be married and . . .

Maud (*breaking away*) Oh no—don't say that!

Verner. How come?

Maud (*moving down L*) I don't want there to be any set plans or arrangements or contracts. This isn't a business deal. Come live with me and be my love for just so long as it works, for just so long as it makes us both happy.

Verner (*moving to below the C chair*) But, honey . . .

Maud. Please, darling Buffalo Bill. We don't want to shackle ourselves with promises before we start. Don't let any sense of moral responsibility rub the gilt off our gingerbread. You do realize, don't you, what a shindy there's going to be? Anna-Mary will scream blue murder. It will be all over Europe and America that Verner Conklin, the millionaire, has left his wife flat and run off with a dubious Italian Princess who runs a shop in Rome and hasn't a penny to her name.

Verner. I didn't know you ran a shop?

Maud. Didn't you? It's quite a success really. We sell curious, rather out-of-the-way things, furniture and whatnots and peculiar jewellery. It's called *La Boutique Fantasque*. That's one of the reasons I have to be back tomorrow. (*She looks at her watch again*) I must go, darling. I must fly like the wind, if I'm to be back by twelve-thirty. (*She collects her bag and coat*)

(Verner *follows her up* C *and helps her on with her coat*)

Don't forget your passport. Oh! (*She looks suddenly stricken*) What about Anna-Mary? What are you going to say to her?

Verner. Nothing much. Just "Good night, sweetheart". It's what I've been saying to her for nineteen years.

MAUD. You're not going to explain? You're not going to tell her anything?

VERNER. What would be the sense of explaining? She'll find out in good time.

MAUD (*conscious-stricken again*) Will she mind? Really mind, I mean?

VERNER. You bet your sweet ass she'll mind. She'll be so hopping mad she'll eat up the furniture.

MAUD. Oh, Verner!

VERNER. Don't you worry about Anna-Mary. It's about time she had a real problem to yak about. (*He opens the door* c) Get going, baby, and be back in that little old Volkswagen at twelve-thirty sharp.

MAUD. Okay, pal! Oh, a thousand times okay!

(MAUD *kisses him, then runs quickly out up* c. VERNER *closes the door and thumps on it twice. Then he goes to the telephone and lifts the receiver*)

VERNER. Hallo, operator? . . . Give me the bar, please. (*He waits for a moment or two, biting his lip thoughtfully*) Hallo, is that the bar? . . . This is Mr Conklin in three-five-four . . . Yeah, I know she's there, but I don't want you to disturb her . . . No, there's no need to say I phoned. Is the party still going on? . . . Uh-uh. The Prince left over an hour ago? I see . . . It's breaking up right now? Thanks—thanks a lot. (*He puts the receiver down, thinks for a moment, then takes off his tie and jacket and puts them over the desk chair. He picks up his book and lies down on the sofa, with his head to* R *and the book on his stomach*)

(ANNA-MARY *enters* c. *She is resplendent in a gown of sapphire-blue satin. She is also wearing a sapphire necklace, ear-rings and a thick bracelet to match. She carries a handbag and a pair of long white gloves. Her expression is grim.* VERNER *snores as she enters.* ANNA-MARY'S *expression becomes grimmer as she sees him asleep*)

ANNA-MARY (*sharply, stamping her foot*) Verner! (*She closes the door*)

VERNER (*waking elaborately*) Why, sweetheart—are you back already?

ANNA-MARY (*disagreeably*) What do you mean—already? It's five of twelve.

VERNER (*sitting up*) Well, who'd have thought it? I guess I must have dropped off.

ANNA-MARY (*putting her bag and gloves on the table by the chair down* L) Dropped off ! You were snoring like a bull moose.

VERNER. I must have been on my back, then. I always snore when I sleep on my back.

ANNA-MARY (*with sarcasm*) That's very interesting, Verner, very interesting indeed. (*She moves below the sofa and waves Verner off*) But you'd better go and snore in your own room now. I'm tired.

(Verner *rises.* Anna-Mary *sinks down in his place*)

Verner. Can I fix you a drink?
Anna-Mary. Yes. A bourbon on the rocks.

(Verner *collects Maud's glass from the* c *table, goes to the drinks table and pours Anna-Mary's drink.* Anna-Mary *kicks off her shoes and puts her feet up on the* r *end of the sofa*)

These shoes have been murder all the evening. They get me right across the instep.
Verner. How was the party?
Anna-Mary. I just wouldn't know, Verner. I'm so darned mad I can't see straight.
Verner. What's wrong?
Anna-Mary. Mariette! That's what's wrong. I'll never speak to her again as long as I live. She's nothing more nor less than a snake-in-the-grass.
Verner (*handing her the drink*) What did she do?
Anna-Mary. Do? She just monopolized the Prince all evening long. I put him on my right naturally, and her on the other side of him and she never gave me the chance to say two words to him.
Verner. Who did you have on your other side?
Anna-Mary. That stuffed shirt Sir Gerard Nutfield. He's got one of those British accents that I just can't stand. He kept asking me where I *came* from. (*Handing him her glass*) Put some more water in that, it's too strong.
Verner (*taking the glass to the drinks table*) Okay, sweetheart. (*He puts water in it and brings it back to her*)
Anna-Mary. My, you look terrible! With no tie on and your hair all mussed up.
Verner. I'll have it set and waved first thing in the morning.
Anna-Mary. I suppose that was meant to be funny.
Verner (*chuckling*) Yes, Anna-Mary, that was supposed to be funny. But—oh boy!—there's better to come! (*He sits on the chair* c *and lights a cigarette*)
Anna-Mary. Have you been drinking?
Verner. Yeah. Like a fish. A golden fish.
Anna-Mary (*coldly*) And what, may I ask, does that mean?
Verner. It means a hell of a lot of things. A kid riding on a dolphin, for instance.
Anna-Mary. *What?*
Verner (*pursuing his dream*) 'And a flat rock and a little white beach and no tie and my hair mussed up.

ANNA-MARY. You've just gone clean out of your mind.

VERNER (*cheerfully*) Way way out. Drink up your booze, ma'am, and enjoy yourself.

ANNA-MARY. How often have I got to tell you that I just can't stand the word "booze", Verner? It's vulgar and it grates on my nerves. You said it to Maud this evening, and I was mortified.

VERNER. *She* didn't seem to mind. Maybe her nerves ain't as sensitive as yours.

ANNA-MARY. I should think not, considering the sort of life she leads. You should have heard what Clare Pethrington was telling me about her tonight. I just couldn't believe my ears.

VERNER. That's the one with buck teeth that we had lunch with today, isn't it?

ANNA-MARY. Verner!

VERNER. She looked as if she could eat an apple through a tennis racket.

ANNA-MARY. I'll have you know that Clare Pethrington is a highly cultured woman. She comes from one of the finest families in England. Her grandfather was the Earl of Babbercome and her great-grandfather was a close friend of Queen Victoria's. He used to stay at Balmor*al* every year, regular as clockwork.

VERNER. Bully for him.

ANNA-MARY. Just because she didn't throw herself at your head and butter you up and make you think how wonderful you were, like Maud did, you think it's funny to make snide remarks about her.

VERNER (*with deceptive gentleness*) I wouldn't like to make any snide remarks about any of your friends, Anna-Mary, but I would like to say, kind of off the record, that in my opinion this dame we happen to be talking about is a snooty, loud-mouthed, bad-mannered bitch.

ANNA-MARY. Verner Conklin. I just *don't want* to talk to you any more. And that's the truth. I just don't want to talk to you *any more!* I come back worn out after an exhausting evening and find you lying here drunk. Then you start making silly jokes and saying mean things about people I respect and admire. I'll tell you here and now I've had just about enough of it. You've changed lately, Verner, and it's no use pretending you haven't. You've changed beyond all recognition.

VERNER. You hit it right on the nose, baby. I sure have.

ANNA-MARY. You'd better go to your room, order some black coffee, and take an Alka-Seltzer.

VERNER (*rising, gaily*) Okay, sweetheart. (*He picks up his jacket and tie and moves back to* c) Did his Serene Highness enjoy his god-damned cigars?

ANNA-MARY (*sitting up straight. Furiously*) Go away, Verner. Go away and leave me alone.

Verner. Okay—okay. That's just exactly what I'm going to do. (*He opens the door* c) Good night, sweetheart.

Verner look at her quizzically for a split second, then goes swiftly out of the room. Anna-Mary sits glaring after him balefully, as—

the Curtain *falls*

FURNITURE AND PROPERTY LIST

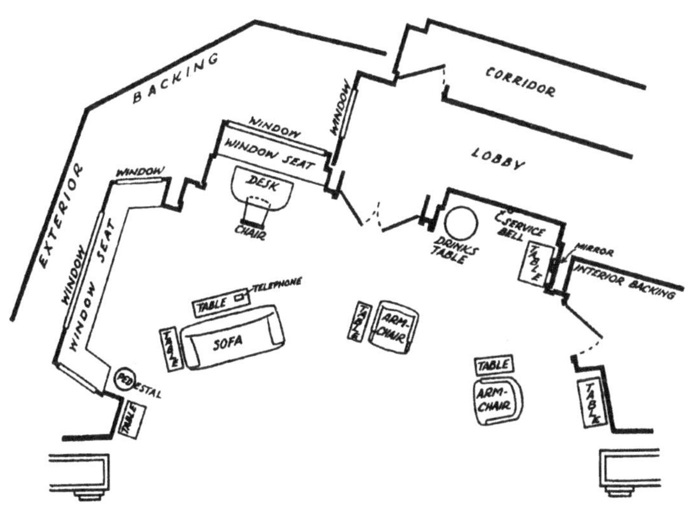

SCENE I

On stage: Sofa (RC) *On it:* cushions
Armchair (C)
Small armchair (down LC)
Desk (up RC) *On it:* writing materials
Desk chair
Sofa-table. *On it:* telephone, cigarette-box (full), lighter, ash-tray, telephone pad, directory
Table (C) *On it:* cigarette-box (full), lighter
Table (down LC) *On it:* cigarette-box (full), lighter
Drinks table (up LC) *On it:* bourbon, gin, Scotch, brandy, vodka, sherry, champagne, soda-water, water, glasses, bottle-opener. *Under it:* wastepaper-basket
On wall up L: mirror
On floor up L, *on desk, window-seat, ad lib.:* flower-baskets
On sofa: sponge-bag

Off stage: Golf clubs (VERNER)
Ice-bucket on tray (FELIX)
Box of cigars (VERNER)

Personal: ANNA-MARY: nail-polisher, cotton wool
MAUD: wristwatch

SCENE 2

Strike: Glasses
Cigar-box

Set: Dinner-trolley in window
James Bond book on sofa

Check: Windows closed
Doors closed

Off stage: Bottle of Evian water in ice on tray (FELIX)

Personal: VERNER: roll of fifty-dollar bills

LIGHTING PLOT

Property fittings required: wall brackets

Interior. A sitting-room

THE APPARENT SOURCES OF LIGHT are: by day, windows R and up RC; by night, wall brackets

THE MAIN ACTING AREAS are down RC, C, down LC, down L

SCENE 1. Evening

To open: Effect of early summer evening light

Cue 1   MAUD exits up C   (Page 16)
Quick fade to black-out

SCENE 2. Night

To open: Black-out

Cue 2   On CURTAIN up   (Page 17)
Quick fade up to night lighting
Blue outside windows. Brackets on

EFFECTS PLOT

SCENE 1

Cue 1   VERNER: "Okay—okay . . ."   (Page 4)
        Telephone rings

Cue 2   ANNA-MARY: ". . . what you're talking about"   (Page 11)
        Telephone rings

SCENE 2

Cue 3   VERNER takes a cigarette   (Page 19)
        Telephone rings

Printed in Great Britain by
Latimer Trend & Company Ltd, Plymouth

www.ingramcontent.com/pod-product-compliance
Ingram Content Group UK Ltd.
Pitfield, Milton Keynes, MK11 3LW, UK
UKHW021817150726
7214IPUK00017B/176